Johannes Walder

A strategic analysis of Ryanair

GRIN Verlag

Bibliografische Information der Deutschen Nationalbibliothek:

Die Deutsche Bibliothek verzeichnet diese Publikation in der Deutschen National-
bibliografie; detaillierte bibliografische Daten sind im Internet über http://dnb.d-
nb.de/ abrufbar.

Imprint:

Copyright © 2012 GRIN Verlag GmbH
Druck und Bindung: Books on Demand GmbH, Norderstedt Germany
ISBN: 978-3-656-40582-5

This book at GRIN:

http://www.grin.com/en/e-book/212378/a-strategic-analysis-of-ryanair

Individual report

A strategic analysis of Ryanair

28th November 2012

I Content

II Figures:

1. Passenger number development in millions from 1995 to 2007

III Abbreviations:

CEO = chief executive officer

FY = fiscal year

USA = United States of America

SWOT = Strengths Weaknesses Opportunities Threats

PR = public relations

1. Introduction

Ryanair was founded in 1985 as a family business. In 1991 Michael O'Leary took over the position as new CEO and adapted the corporate strategy after the model of Southwest Airlines in the USA. Success proved him right: Ryanairs' passenger numbers (figure 1) have increased steadily confirming his choice of strategy.

This paper will analyse the reason behind the decision for low cost leadership as corporate strategy. Furthermore the implementation of the strategy into their value chain is going to be described and finally it is going to be evaluated if the strategy was successful.

Figure 1: Passenger number development in millions from 1995 to 2007

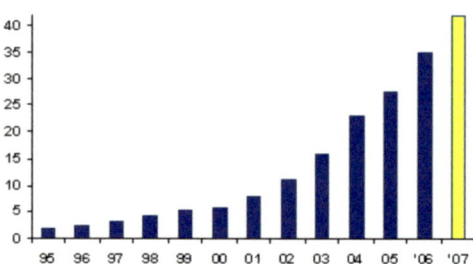

Source: http://www.ryanair.com/en/about, accessed on 04.11.2012

2. Analysis of the internal and external factors (SWOT)

The internal and external factors that led to Ryanairs' strategic choice can be found in the SWOT analysis. A SWOT analysis provides a description of the external business environment in the form of opportunities and threats, and it presents the strategic capabilities of the organization in the form of strengths and weaknesses. This analysis can be used as a foundation for strategic options. However, a SWOT is best used in comparison with other companies to get a relative view of your situation (Johnson G. et all, 2008).

2.1 Strengths

Ryanair profits from their charismatic and polarizing leadership of their CEO Michael O'Leary. He brought the knowledge of the business model of Southwest Airlines and applied it consequently in the company. Without him the cost leadership strategy would not have been implemented. He also promotes Ryanair at every possible opportunity and creates a lot of media attention (Jonathan Hemus, 2012).

2.2 Weaknesses

Ryanair's main weakness was their lack of efficiency. Slow turnarounds and high operating costs made them a small competitor compared to the Aer Lingus. This lack of efficiency manifests itself in the fact that they weren't profitable.

2.3 Opportunities

The European deregulation posed as a huge opportunity for Ryanair since the market in Europe was easier to access for the company. Expansion and growth to other countries and airports was made less complicated.

2.4 Threats

The threats for Ryanair were mainly their competitors. Increasing competition also due to the deregulation posed a considerable threat to the rather small company.

3. Strategic options for Ryanair

When the new CEO Michael O'Leary took office he faced a company which wasn't profitable and had no clear strategy. He had several options which will be outlined in the following by using the VRIO method. This method is used to evaluate a strategy based on the four factors, value, rarity, imitability and organization (Barney et al, 2005).

3.1 Merger

One strategy for Ryanair would have been to merge with another competitor such as Aer Lingus to gain additional market share, safe costs due to synergies and strengthen their capital base. This strategy would create value for the reasons mentioned above and would be rather rare since there aren't many mergers in the airline industry. Furthermore, it would be difficult to imitate since a merger is very delicate. However, Ryanair didn't have the financial resources to conduct this strategy in a benefitting way.

3.2 Premium strategy

Another option would have been to focus on the premium segment and therefore business customers. This strategy would create more value for the business since companies tend to let their employees fly the more expensive business class. Still, the strategy isn't rare since there are lots of competitors in that market segment already for example British Airways. Ryanair also didn't have the necessary financial resources to upgrade their fleet in terms of bigger planes, better equipment and more staff.

3.3 Cost leadership

The chosen strategy however was to gain a competitive advantage through low cost leadership. This would create value due to the lower operating costs and the additional customers attracted by the low prices. Furthermore, this strategy was rare - Ryanair was the first to set up a budget airline in Europe and had the first mover advantage in terms of brand recognition. In addition is also costly to imitate as the strategy relies on having no hubs, which all the other airlines heavily relied on. The strategy of low cost leadership also requires low wages for the staff which is more difficult in unionized areas like Spain or Scandinavia. Ryanair had the necessary organizational capabilities, because they were relatively small compared to the major airlines and could adjust more quickly. Additionally, Ryanair had a CEO who was willing to implement his knowledge of Southwest airlines to create a competitive advantage.

O'Leary chose that option because he had seen it being deployed successfully by Southwest Airlines in the USA. Ryanair was pushed out of the premium market by their competitors. The easy access to the European market due to the deregulation and the lack of a real low cost carrier airline opened up a niche for Ryanair to become the first in the market.

4. Implementation

The implementation of the low cost strategy will be explained using the value chain model created by Michael Porter (1998). The value chain shows what activities a company performs to deliver a product or a service to the customer. Michael Porter created this model to make it easier to depict where exactly the strategic advantage lies within a company's structure (Porter, 1998). Ryanair is applying its' no frills strategy on every step of the value chain.

The inbound logistics or service providers in form of the secondary airports that Ryanair flies to are cheaper and less crowded than the major airports in big cities. This gives Ryanair the advantage of having lower costs and quicker turnarounds since they can operate the airport alone.

The operations of Ryanair, like baggage handling and inflight services are mostly being charged on the customer in form of extra fees. Examples of the services not included in the ticket price are luggage check in or drinks during the flight.

Outbound logistic are not relevant for Ryanair as they are the final service provider and they do not offer services for customers after the flight is over (except for the return of the luggage).

Their marketing is majorly driven by Michael O'Leary himself as he uses every opportunity to create PR for Ryanair for example in interviews (Hemus, 2012).

The service that Ryanair provides is limited and stripped down to the bare essentials. Ryanair charges extra fees for everything that goes beyond travelling without luggage. Furthermore, costs are kept low by preventing unions who could go on strike for higher wages. The service personnel on the plane is also cleaning the plane after a flight; a service which most of the other big airlines outsource to external firms. This, however, safes not only personnel costs but also makes quick turnarounds possible which allow Ryanair to use their fleet more efficiently. The whole company also profits from the relatively low corporation tax rate (12,5%) in Ireland compared to other European countries (ec.europa.eu). Ryanair also hedges 80% of their oil prices in FY 2012 in order to avoid raising the ticket prices. Other airlines put levies on their tickets to cope with rising costs but Ryanair chose a riskier strategy in order to keep its competitive advantage of low prices (Ryanair Q3 results, 2011). As a result the ticket prices can be kept low and the competitive advantage towards their competition sustained.

5. Strategic analysis of Ryanair

Ryanair profits from its clear business strategy. According to Richard Rumelt (1993) there are four aspects which a strategy has to provide to be an acceptable choice for the management. First, it has to provide consistency, meaning that the strategy shouldn't have several mutual exclusive goals. The second is consonance, which means that the strategy has to adapt to external factors and at the same time be able to compete with other companies who are also adapting. The third aspect is the advantage it has to provide. It should be focused and based on gaining a competitive advantage. And finally it should be feasible concerning the internal capabilities and resources of the company (Rumelt, 1993).

The internal consistency of the strategy can be seen by Michael O'Leary's statement on their website about their low operating costs. In the statement called strategy it is stated that the Ryanair management will focus on reducing the four primary sources of costs being aircraft equipment costs, personnel costs, customer service costs and airport access and handling costs (www.ryanair.com).

The consonance of its strategy is seen as they discovered the apparent need for a low cost airline in Europe and adjusted their strategy accordingly. Also when competitors lower their prices Ryanair does too.

The competitive advantage of their strategy is created by Ryanairs' low fares which other airlines have failed to match and their first mover advantage in the low cost market.

The Low cost strategy was also feasible as Ryanair had the necessary resources and abilities to implement the strategy in their company. The low corporate tax in Ireland, their lack of unions and the determination of their CEO gave way for the successful execution of their strategy.

6. Conclusion

In conclusion, Ryanair has chosen strategy that gave them a sustained competitive advantage until today.

The company's no-frills strategy combined with the decision to only work with secondary airports, to fly point to point instead of using big hubs like Heathrow and their choice to focus on short hauls instead of long distance transcontinental flights made their cost leadership strategy successful. The implementation of their strategy was very effective as it covered every step of their value chain.

As a recommendation the author would suggest a continuing focus on the cost leadership and further development of chargeable services on flight like online gambling or in flight video streaming.

References

In alphabetical order

1. Jay Barney and William Hesterly, 2005, Strategic Management and Competitive Advantage: Concepts; Pearson Education, Inc., Upper Saddle River, New Jersey
2. Richard Berstein, 2003, An Aging Europe May Find Itself on the Sidelines http://www.nytimes.com/2003/06/29/world/an-aging-europe-may-find-itself-on-the-sidelines.html?pagewanted=all&src=pm; accessed on 13.11.2012
3. K. Capell, 2003, Ryanair Rising: Ireland's discount carrier is defying gravity as the industry struggles, Business Week, 3835, 30.
4. Jonathan Hemus, 2012, How Ryanair's Michael O'Leary Turns Every Media Interview Into an Opportunity http://www.business2community.com/strategy/how-ryanairs-michael-oleary-turns-every-media-interview-into-an-opportunity-0319970#ut7pof1FIShu8Mal.99, accessed on 07.11.2012
5. Gerry Johnson, Richard Whittington, Kevan Scholes, 2007, Exploring Corporate Strategy: Text and Cases, Financial Times/ Prentice Hall; 8th edition
6. Michael Porter, 1998, Competitive Advantage: Creating and Sustaining Superior Performance, Free Press
7. **Updated version of** Richard Rumelt, 1993, Evaluating business strategy in William Glueck, 1980, *Strategic Management and Business Policy*, McGrawHill, New York
8. http://www.fedprimerate.com/crude-oil-price-history.htm; accessed on 04.11.2012
9. http://ec.europa.eu/taxation_customs/tedb/taxDetail.html?id=324/1328227200&taxType=CIT, accessed on 04.11.2012
10. Ryanair Ltd., Annual Report 2011, Dublin

6

11. http://www.ryanair.com/en/news/ryanair-no-1customer-service-stats-february-2011, accessed on 04.11.2012

12. Ryanair Holdings PLC RYA 3rd Quarter Results, 31st of January 2011, Bloomberg http://www.bloomberg.com/apps/news?pid=newsarchive&sid=akX4QvW49aDE ,accessed on 08.11.2012

13. www.ryanair.com/doc/investor/Strategy.pdf , accessed on 08.11.2012, Strategy